Praise Hits
Complete Level 1
For the Later Beginner

Arranged by Tom Gerou, Gayle Kowalchyk, and E. L. Lancaster

 Alfred

Produced by
Alfred Music
P.O. Box 10003
Van Nuys, CA 91410-0003
alfred.com

Printed in USA.

ISBN-10: 1-4706-1957-1
ISBN-13: 978-1-4706-1957-2

Foreword

This series answers the often expressed need for contemporary Christian music to be used as supplementary pieces for students. Soon after beginning piano study, students can play attractive versions of the best-known praise music of today.

This book is correlated page-by-page with Lesson Book, Complete Level 1 of *Alfred's Basic Piano Library*; pieces should be assigned based on the instructions in the upper-right corner of each title page of *Praise Hits*. Since the melodies and rhythms of praise music do not always lend themselves to precise grading, you may find that these pieces are sometimes a little longer and more difficult than the corresponding pages in the Lesson Book. The teacher's judgment is the most important factor in deciding when to assign each arrangement.

When the books in the *Praise Hits* series are assigned in conjunction with the Lesson Books, these appealing pieces reinforce new concepts as they are introduced. In addition, the motivation the music provides could not be better. The emotional satisfaction that students receive from mastering each praise song increases their enthusiasm to begin the next one.

Contents

Use with Alfred's Basic Piano Library
Lesson Book Complete Level 1, after page 11.

Praise the Name of Jesus

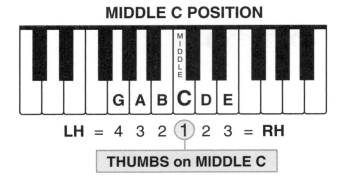

MIDDLE C POSITION

LH = 4 3 2 ① 2 3 = RH

THUMBS on MIDDLE C

Words and Music by Roy Hicks, Jr.
Arr. by Kowalchyk and Lancaster

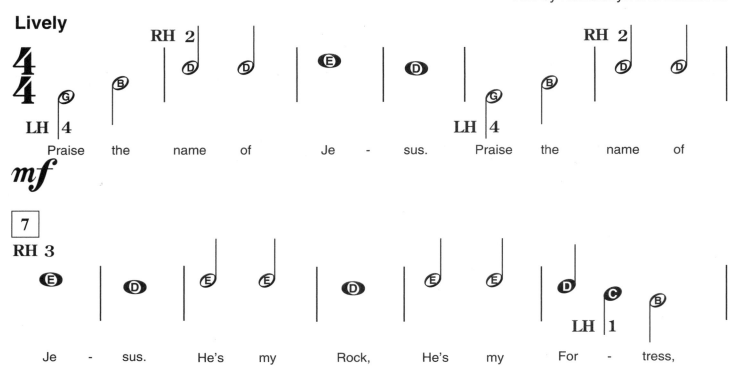

Praise the name of Je - sus. Praise the name of

Je - sus. He's my Rock, He's my For - tress,

DUET PART (Student plays 1 octave higher.)

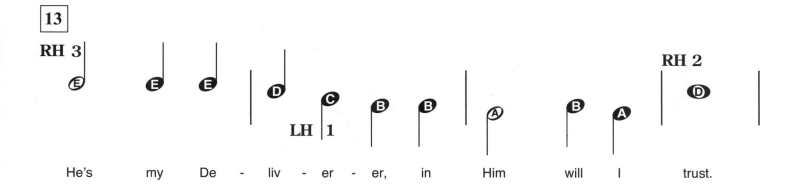

13

RH 3 E E E | D C B B | A B A | RH 2 D |

LH 1

He's my De - liv - er - er, in Him will I trust.

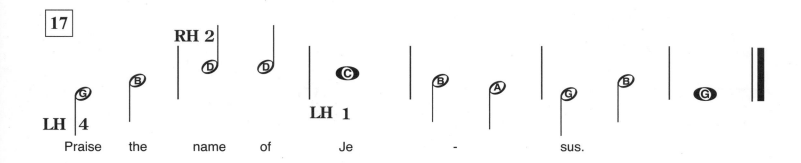

17

RH 2

LH 4 G B | D D | C | B A G B | G ‖

LH 1

Praise the name of Je - - sus.

Use after page 21.

Jesus, Name Above All Names

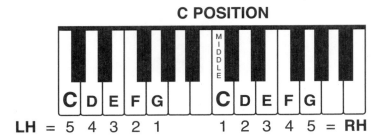

C POSITION

Words and Music by Naida Hearn
Arr. by Kowalchyk and Lancaster

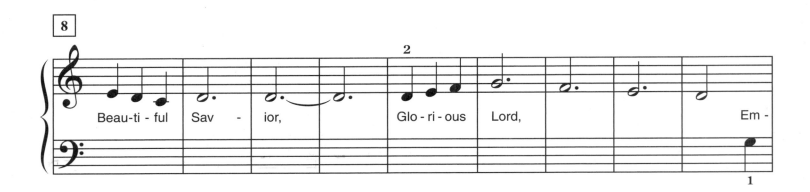

DUET PART (Student plays 1 octave higher.)

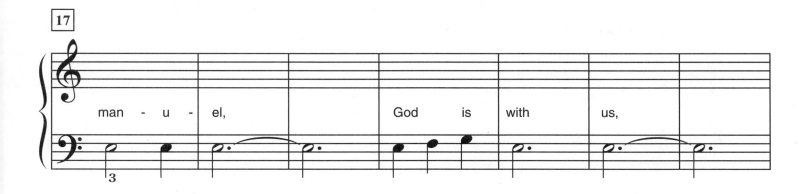

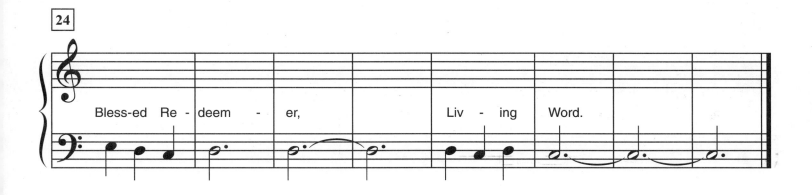

Blessed Be the Lord God Almighty

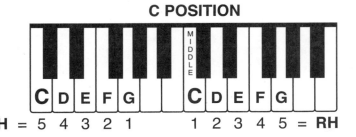

C POSITION

LH = 5 4 3 2 1   1 2 3 4 5 = RH

Words and Music by Bob Fitts
Arr. by Kowalchyk and Lancaster

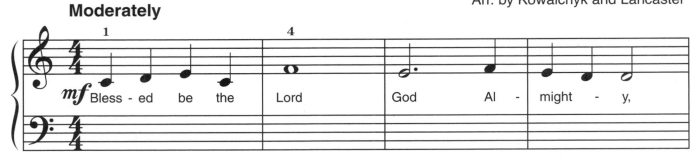

Moderately

Bless-ed be the Lord God Al - might - y,

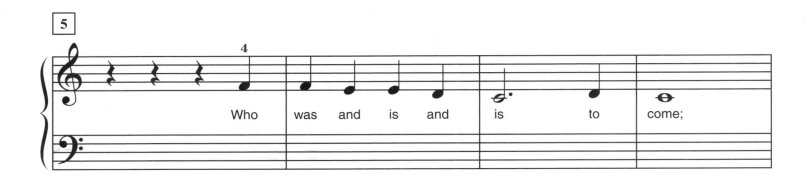

Who was and is and is to come;

DUET PART (Student plays 2 octaves higher.)

Moderately

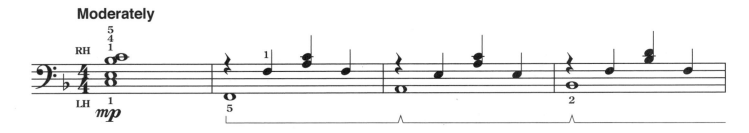

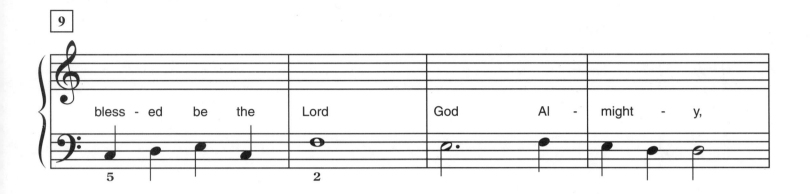

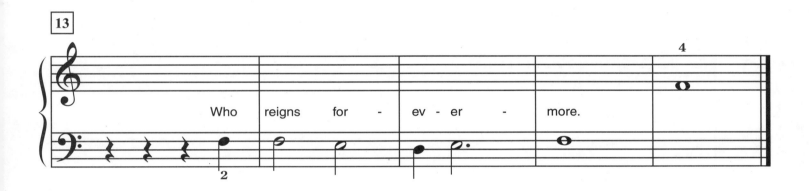

Shout to the North

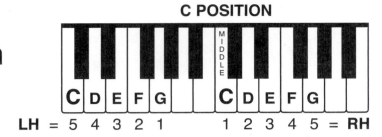

C POSITION

LH = 5 4 3 2 1   1 2 3 4 5 = RH

Words and Music by Martin Smith
Arr. by Kowalchyk and Lancaster

Flowing waltz tempo

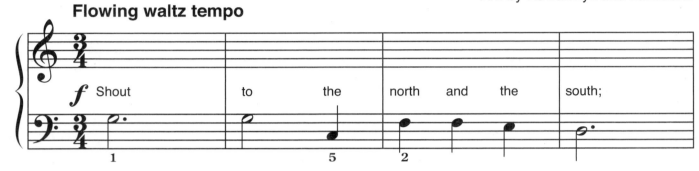

f Shout to the north and the south;

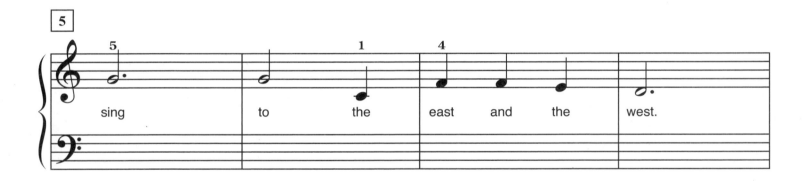

sing to the east and the west.

DUET PART (Student plays 1 octave higher.)

Flowing waltz tempo

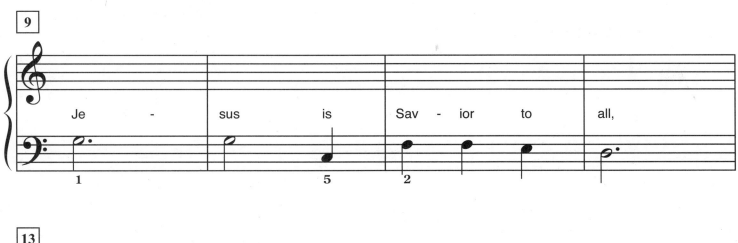

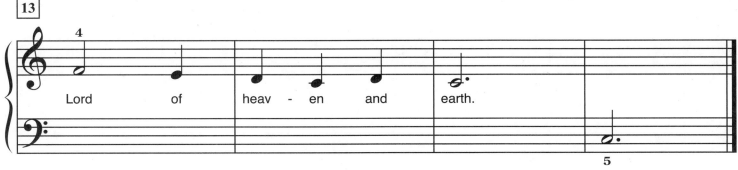

Open the Eyes of My Heart

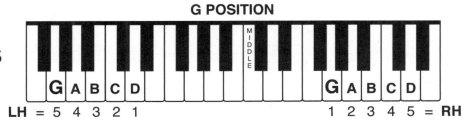

G POSITION

Words and Music by Paul Baloche
Arr. by Kowalchyk and Lancaster

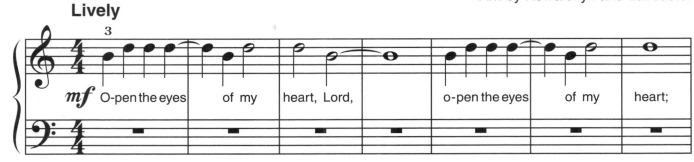

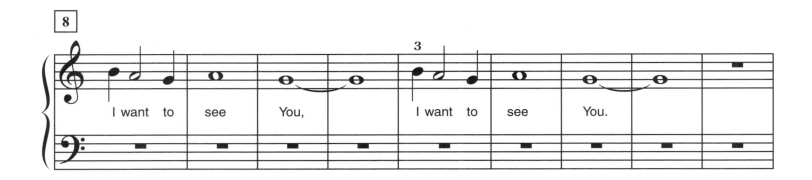

DUET PART (Student plays RH 1 octave higher; LH 2 octaves higher.)

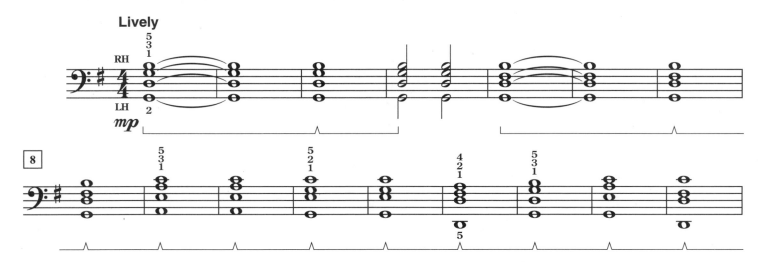

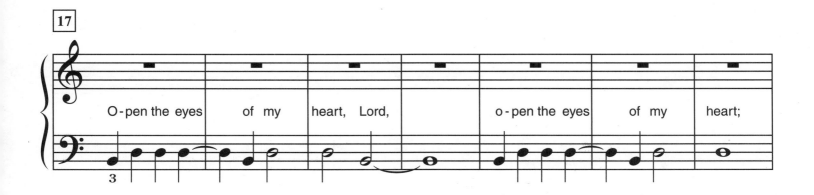

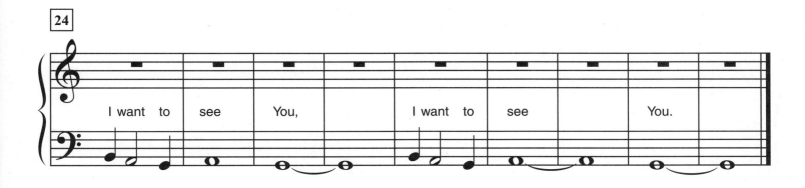

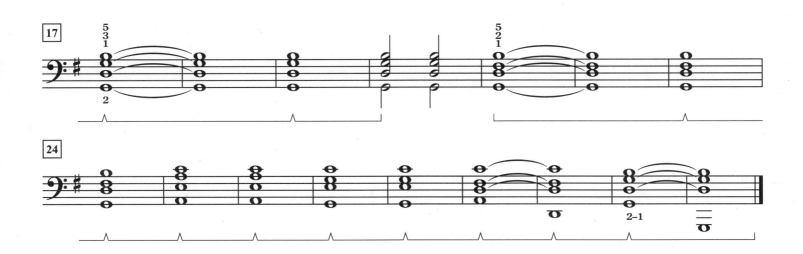

Use after page 34.

There Is None Like You

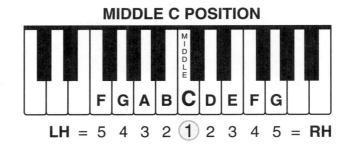

MIDDLE C POSITION

Words and Music by Lenny LeBlanc
Arr. by Kowalchyk and Lancaster

Moderately slow

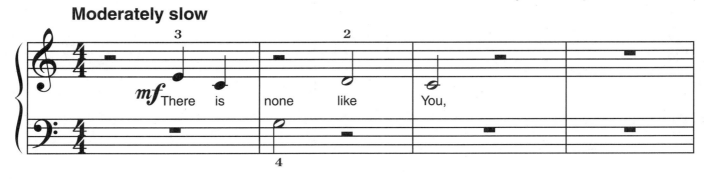

mf There is none like You,

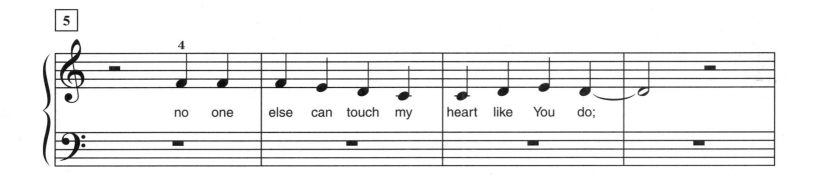

no one else can touch my heart like You do;

DUET PART (Student plays 1 octave higher.)

Moderately slow

mp _simile_

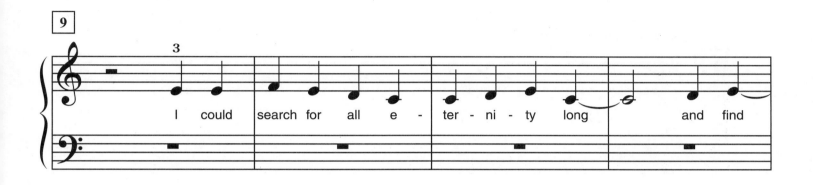

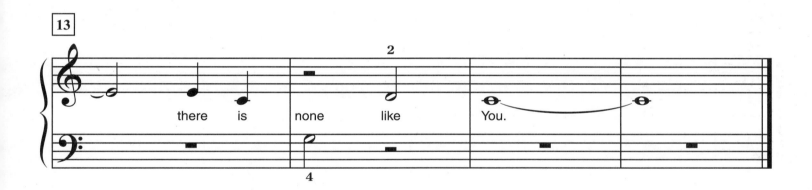

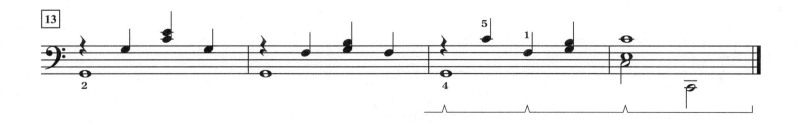

Use after page 35.

Here I Am to Worship
(Light of the World)

C POSITION

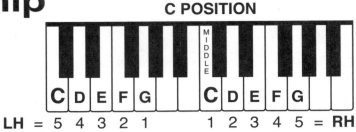

Words and Music by Tim Hughes
Arr. by Kowalchyk and Lancaster

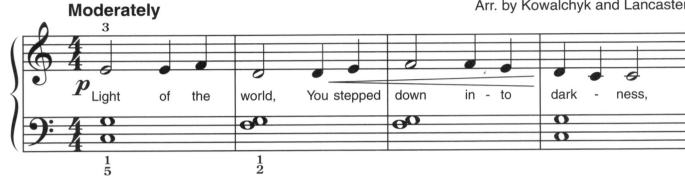

Light of the world, You stepped down in-to dark - ness,

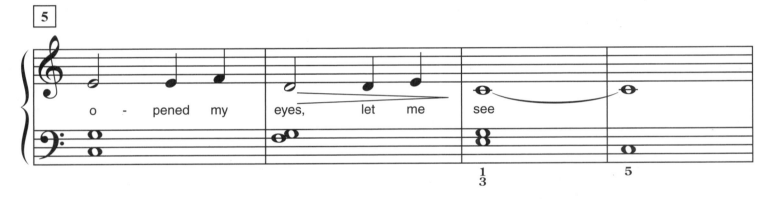

o - pened my eyes, let me see

beau - ty that made this heart a - dore You,

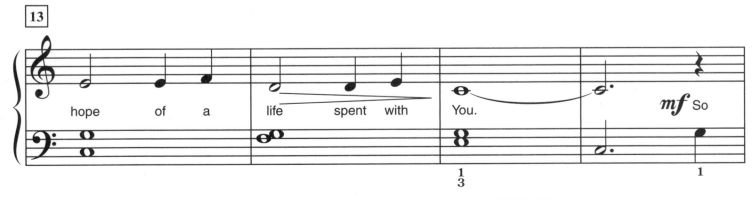

hope of a life spent with You. *mf* So

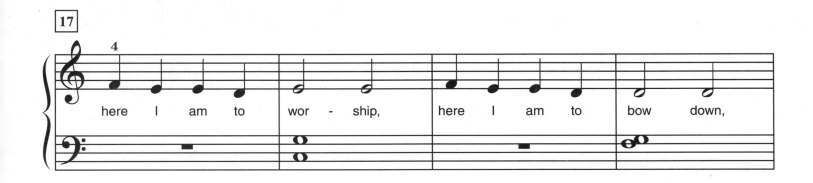

here I am to wor - ship, here I am to bow down,

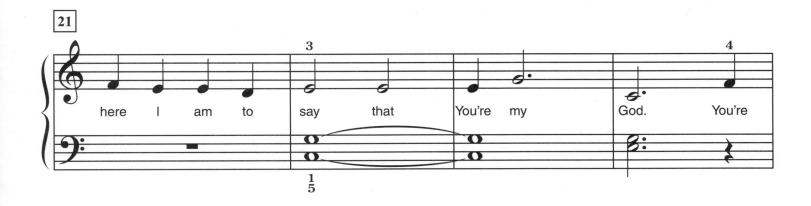

here I am to say that You're my God. You're

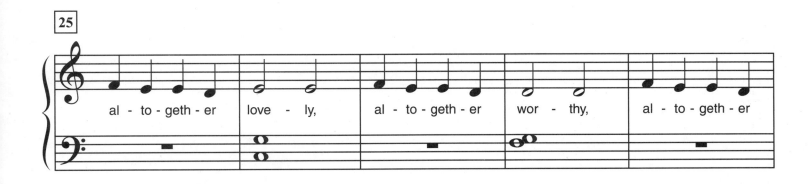

al - to - geth - er love - ly, al - to - geth - er wor - thy, al - to - geth - er

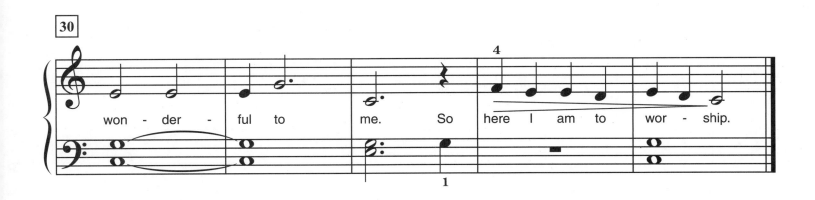

won - der - ful to me. So here I am to wor - ship.

Use after page 41.

Worthy, You Are Worthy

Words and Music by Don Moen
Arr. by Tom Gerou

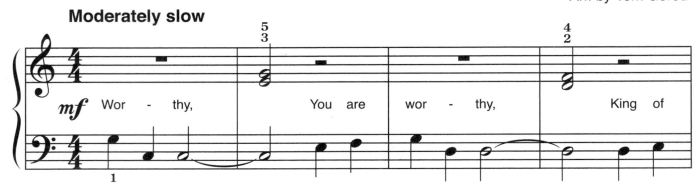

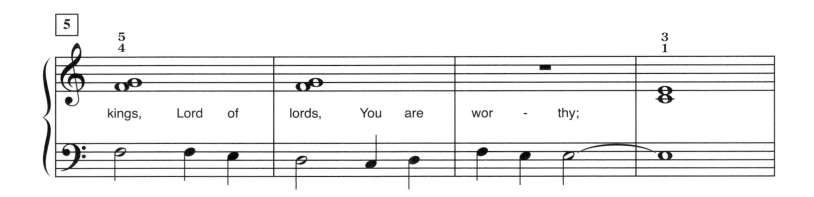

DUET PART (Student plays 1 octave higher.)

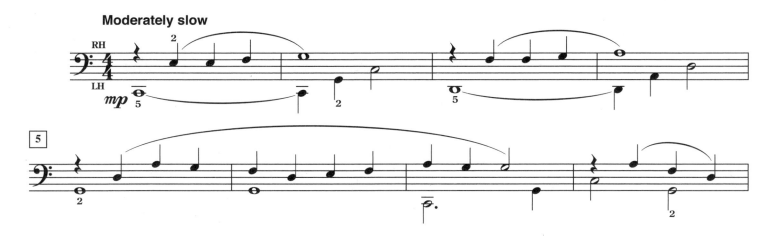

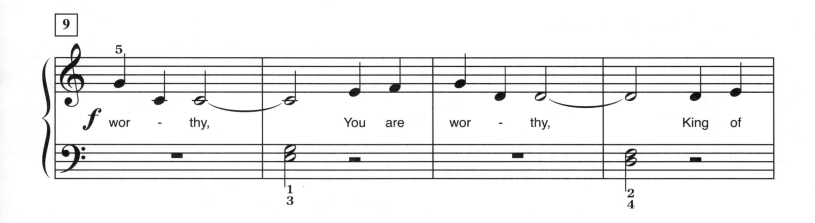

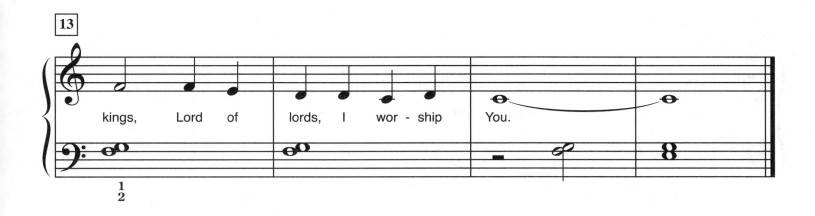

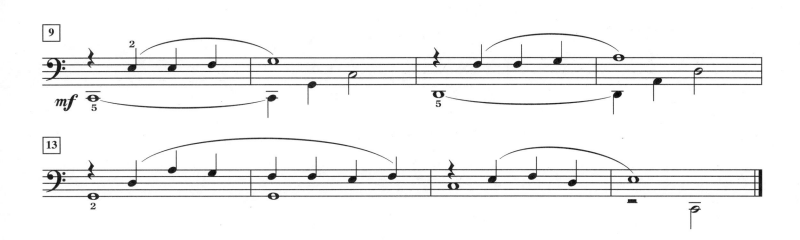

Use after page 42.

Blessed Be the Name of the Lord

Words and Music by Don Moen
Arr. by Tom Gerou

Moderately

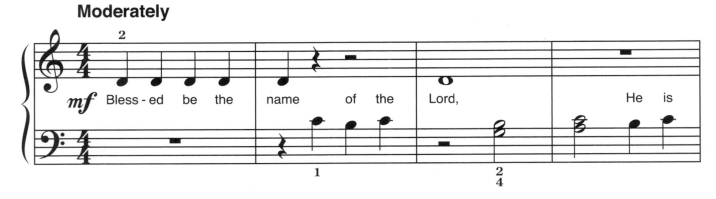

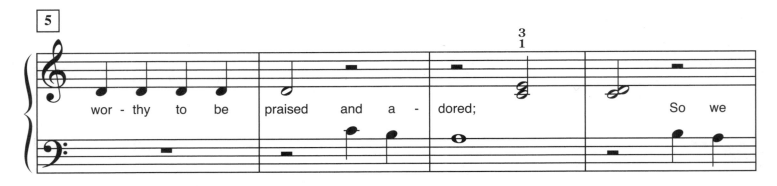

DUET PART (Student plays 1 octave higher.)

Moderately

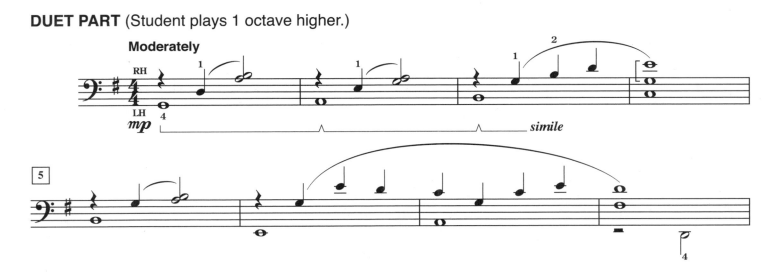

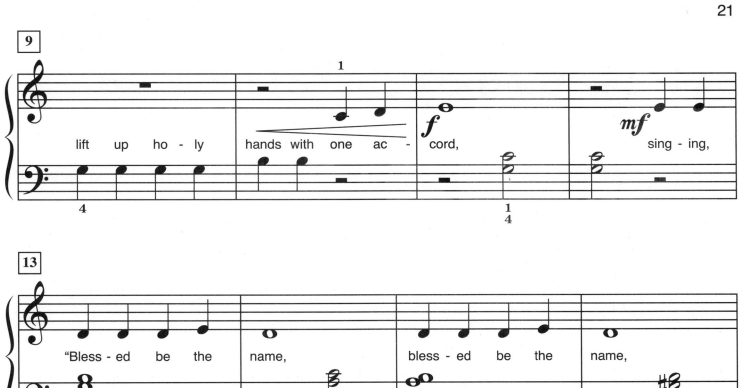

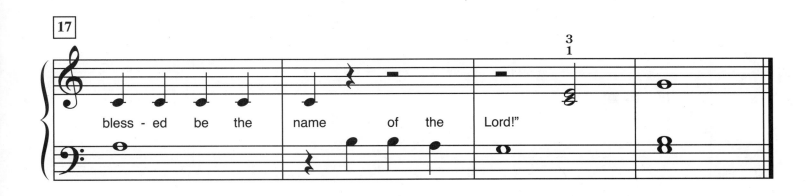

Use after page 45.

More Precious Than Silver

Words and Music by Lynn DeShazo
Arr. by Tom Gerou

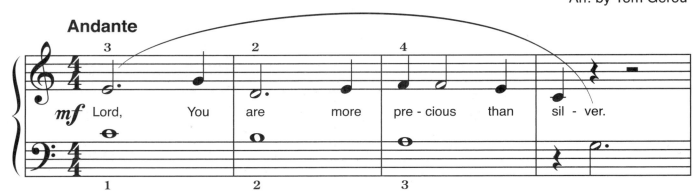

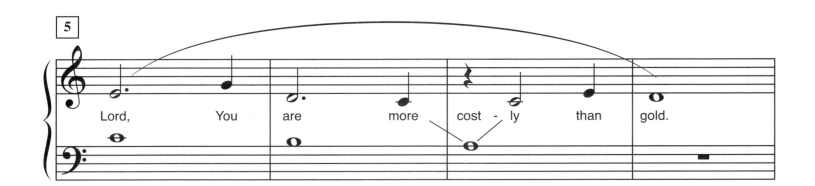

DUET PART (Student plays 1 octave higher.)

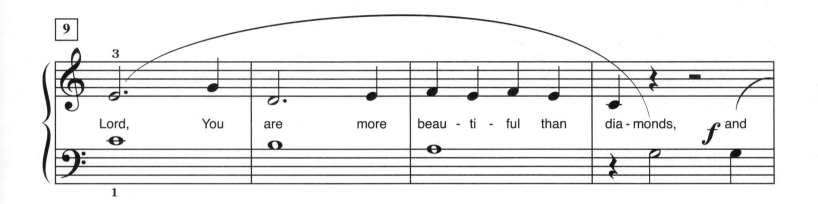

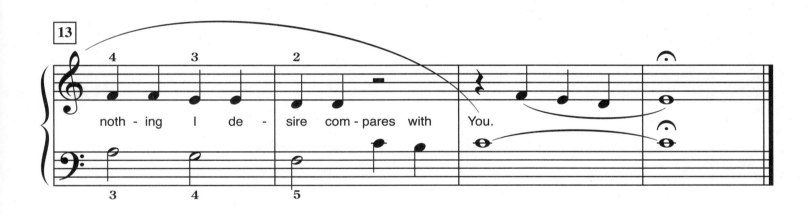

Amazing Grace
(My Chains Are Gone)

Words and Music by
Chris Tomlin and Louie Giglio
Arr. by Tom Gerou

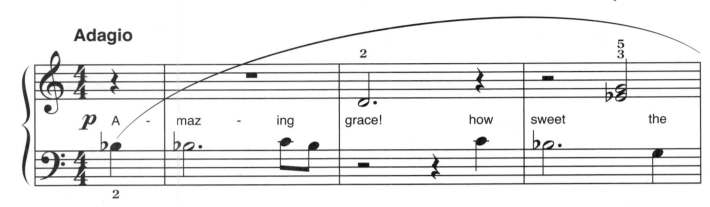

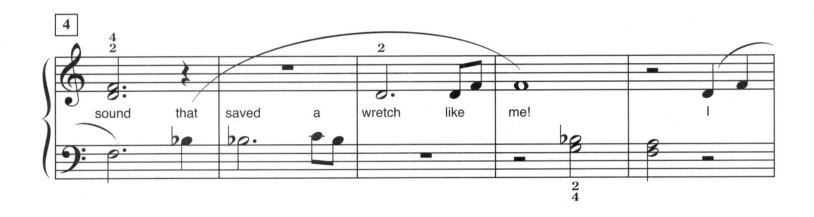

DUET PART (Student plays 1 octave higher.)

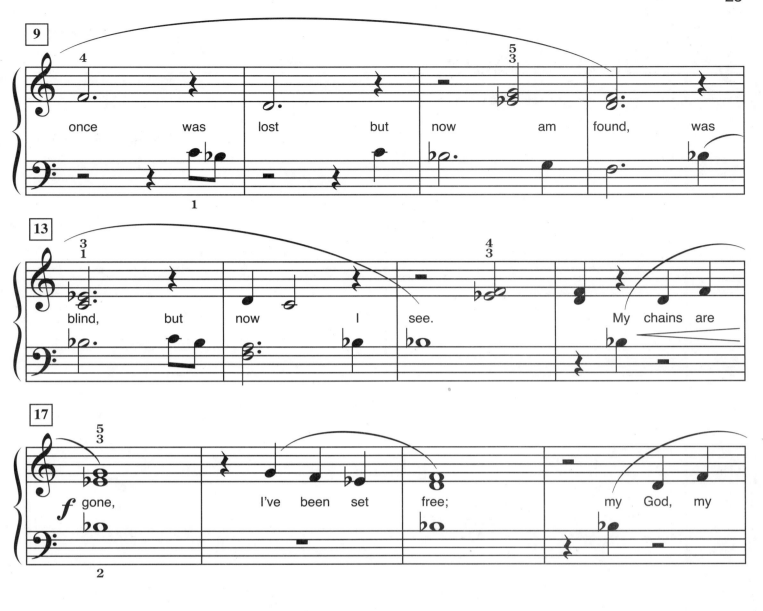

once was lost but now am found, was blind, but now I see. My chains are gone, I've been set free; my God, my

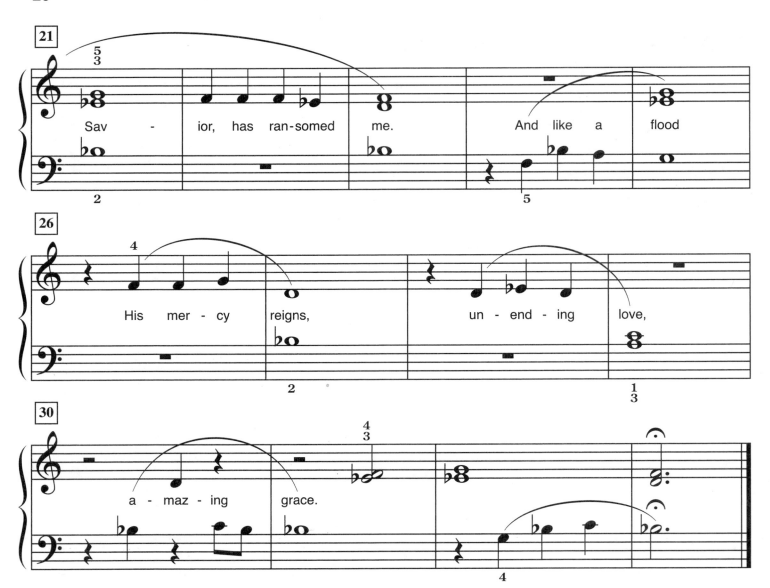

(DUET PART)

You Are My All in All

Words and Music by Dennis L. Jernigan

Arr. by Tom Gerou

DUET PART (Student plays 1 octave higher.)

(DUET PART)

Use after page 54.

Shout to the Lord

Words and Music by Darlene Zschech
Arr. by Tom Gerou

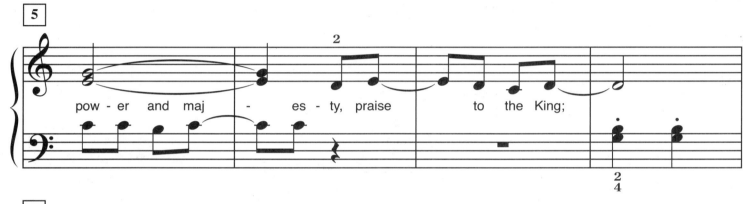

DUET PART (Student plays 1 octave higher.)

Both hands 8va to end

sound of Your Name. I sing for joy

at the work of Your hands; for - ev - er I'll love

You, for - ev - er I'll stand; noth - ing com-pares

to the prom - ise I have in You.

ritardando

ritardando

Use after pages 56–57.

How Great Is Our God

Words and Music by
Jesse Reeves, Chris Tomlin and Ed Cash

Arr. by Tom Gerou

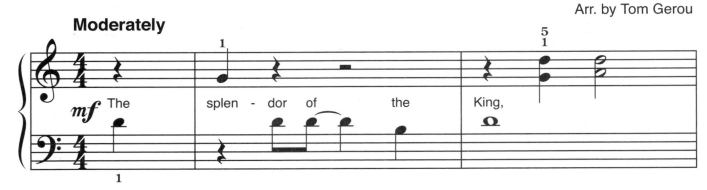

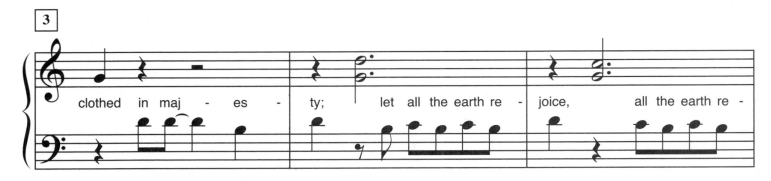

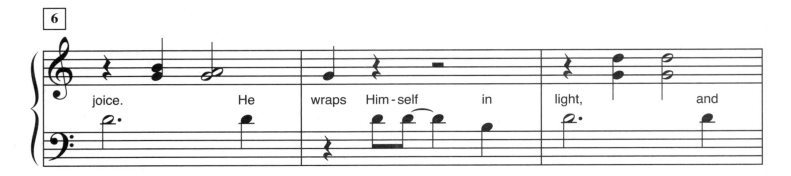

DUET PART (Student plays 1 octave higher.)

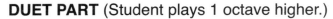

Use after pages 58–59.

As the Deer

Words and Music by Martin Nystrom

Arr. by Tom Gerou

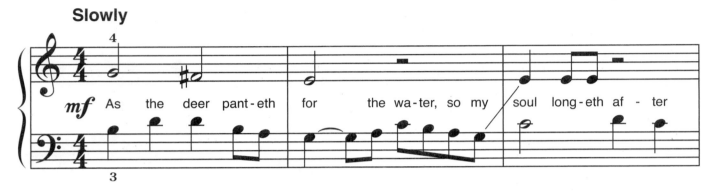

DUET PART (Student plays 1 octave higher.)

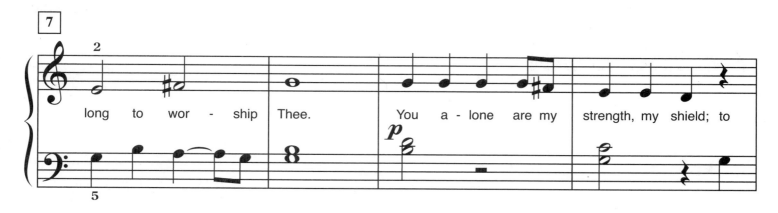

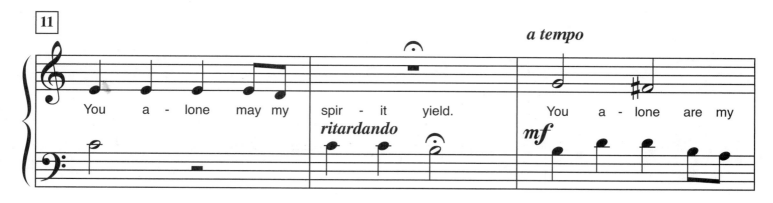

Use after page 66.

Beautiful One

Words and Music by Tim Hughes
Arr. by Tom Gerou

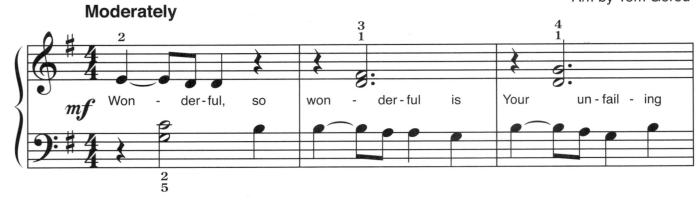

Won - der-ful, so won - der-ful is Your un - fail - ing

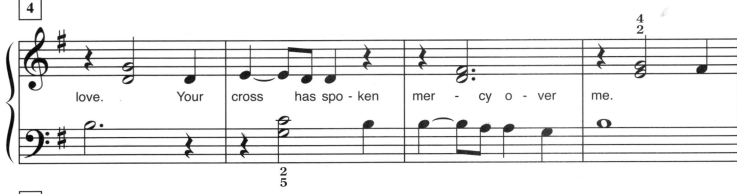

love. Your cross has spo - ken mer - cy o - ver me.

No eye has seen, no ear has heard, no heart could ful - ly

DUET PART (Student plays 1 octave higher.)

Come, Now Is the Time to Worship

Words and Music by Brian Doerksen
Arr. by Tom Gerou

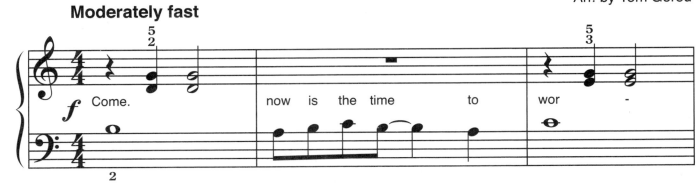

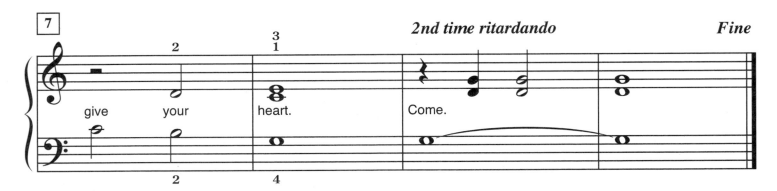

DUET PART (Student plays 1 octave higher.)

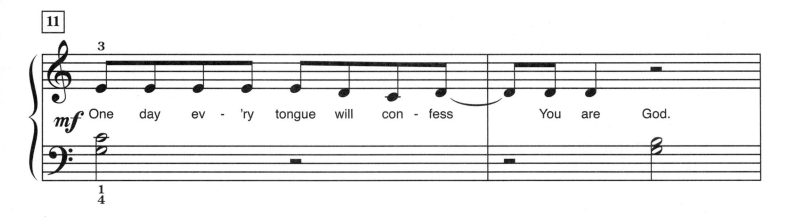

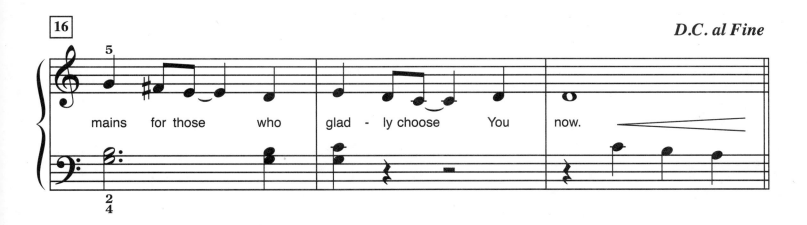

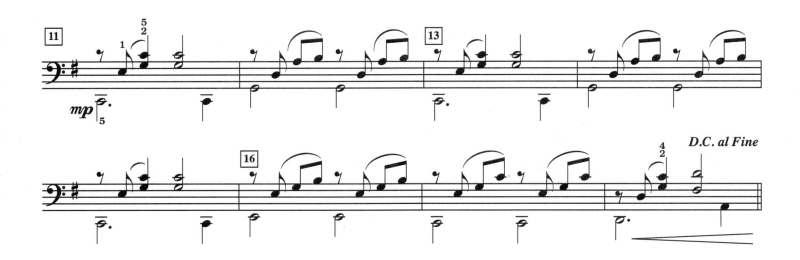

Use after pages 68–69.

Mighty Is Our God

Words and Music by
Don Moen, Eugene Greco and Gerrit Gustafson
Arr. by Tom Gerou

Moderately fast

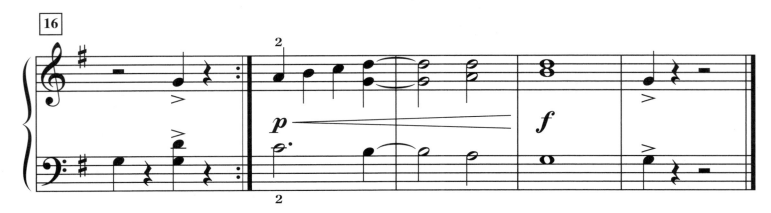